BASKING *in the* SON-SHINE

BASKING
in the
SON-SHINE

Maxine Lantz

WestBow
PRESS
A DIVISION OF THOMAS NELSON

Copyright © 2012 Maxine Lantz

All rights reserved. No part of this book may be used or reproduced by any means, graphic, electronic, or mechanical, including photocopying, recording, taping or by any information storage retrieval system without the written permission of the publisher except in the case of brief quotations embodied in critical articles and reviews.

WestBow Press books may be ordered through booksellers or by contacting:

WestBow Press
A Division of Thomas Nelson
1663 Liberty Drive
Bloomington, IN 47403
www.westbowpress.com
1-(866) 928-1240

Because of the dynamic nature of the Internet, any web addresses or links contained in this book may have changed since publication and may no longer be valid. The views expressed in this work are solely those of the author and do not necessarily reflect the views of the publisher, and the publisher hereby disclaims any responsibility for them.

Certain stock imagery © Thinkstock.
Any people depicted in stock imagery provided by Thinkstock are models, and such images are being used for illustrative purposes only.

ISBN: 978-1-4497-5596-6 (e)
ISBN: 978-1-4497-5595-9 (sc)

Library of Congress Control Number: 2012910391

Printed in the United States of America

WestBow Press rev. date: 9/21/2012

AUTHOR'S FOREWORD

I have called this booklet of poetry "Basking in the Son-Shine" because that is what I do since I yielded my life to Christ. His love warms my life like no other could. I hope that these poems will give you some insight into what I believe is the true character of God and his son, Jesus Christ. I thank God for saving me, and I look forward to spending eternity with God and Jesus Christ.

I pray that these poems will edify the reader, and that those who know Christ as Saviour will be encouraged to continue their walk with him. For the reader that does not yet know Christ in this personal way, I pray that these words will lead you to the point in your life where you will accept Christ as your personal Saviour.

I would also like to take this opportunity to thank the keepers of my words. Each poem I write gets sent to my sister (Lynda Taylor), my husband Jim, my pastor and his wife (John & Cheryl Scorgie, who are also dear friends), and to another two friends (Carrol Ross and Joyce Lindsay). They are my biggest supporters, and I thank them for their love, loyalty and faithfulness.

Thank-you,
Maxine Lantz

Other Books By This Author:

Rhyming Revelation

Love On The Wing

Flights Of Fancy

Covenant Of Care

Abundant Life

CONTENTS

A PASTOR'S PLEA

Lord Jehovah, hear my prayer.
Help me serve those in my care.
Bestow on me, Lord, the ability
To recognize each person's need.
Grant me wisdom, just yours alone,
As to my flock your love is shown.
Let me preach your Word in truth,
So all will see their need of you.
Lord, help me build and edify
Your people, as each day goes by.
Lord, let me never be ashamed
Of calling on your holy name.
Give me boldness, without fear,
For I know you're always near.
Discernment, too, is what I need
To lead this flock, and to succeed.
Lord, may I never count the cost
Of reaching all the world's lost.
And let my own life be the proof
Of all the faithful gifts from you.
So, Father, grant these things I ask
As I perform your appointed task.

A SAINT WENT HOME TO HEAVEN

A saint went home to heaven today;
Her walk on earth is done.
She's walking on those golden paths
With Jesus, God's own son.
She asked Him to be her savior
At the tender age of ten.
She's walked his narrow way and has
Been led by Him since then.

He'd blessed her with a husband
Who loved the Lord as well,
And seven lovely children
To whom His love she'd tell.
And when she'd lost her husband,
Christ held her hand always,
Throughout the lonely hours
And all the lonely days.

When the doctor gave the bad news,
She took it all in stride
For she knew the Lord was with her
And would always walk beside.
The doctors could do nothing more
To slow the cancer's gain,
And all their modern medicine
Ensured she'd feel no pain.

And at the moment of her death,
Her body left behind,
She soared to heaven's pearly gates
And there, her Lord, did find.
The joy that filled her soul that day
No man can understand.
She stood before her Creator King
In heaven's glory land.

A SPIRIT OF UNITY

May the God who gives endurance and encouragement
give you a spirit of unity among yourselves as you follow
Christ Jesus, so that with one heart and mouth you may
glorify the God and Father of our Lord Jesus Christ.

Romans 15:5-6 NIV

A spirit of unity,
Oh Lord, we pray
Is what you would give us
This very day.
You encourage us daily
And endurance impart.
Help us today
To unite all our hearts.
As we follow you, Jesus,
The world will see,
To your glory and honour,
Our unity.
With one heart united,
We'll divide nevermore.
With one mouth, we'll praise you
For evermore.
The Father of our Lord,
Our Savior, our King
Will be glorified by
Our praise offering.
With our hearts united
That the world sees in us,
They may want what they see
And in Christ they will trust.
A spirit of unity,
Oh Lord, we pray
Is what you would give us
This very day.

AS WE WORK AND SERVE

"God is not unjust; he will not forget your work and the love you have shown him as you have helped his people and continue to help them."

Hebrews 6:10 NIV

As we work and serve the Lord,
He won't forget and will reward.
As we show our love to Him,
We won't lack for anything.
As we help the world's lost,
He'll help us not to count the cost.
As we tell of God's great love,
He will bless from up above.
As we just obey and trust,
We will learn God's not unjust.
As we see His faithful ways,
We will praise Him all our days.
As we strive God's love to show,
God's great blessings we will know.
As we learn to never fear,
God will always be right near.
As we look to heaven's gain,
May we hear our God's refrain,
"Time on earth, Child, now is gone.
Faithful servant, welcome home."

BE STILL AND KNOW

"Be still, and know that I am God; I will be exalted among the nations, I will be exalted in the earth."

Psalm 46:10 NIV

Be still and know that I am God.
And don't heed the world's lies.
Its gods have ears that cannot hear,
And all have blinded eyes.

The nations will my name exalt
And all the earth proclaim,
"This God has wisdom, power too,
All held in Jesus' name."

My power alone can save and heal
Available to all
Of those who live in Jesus Christ
And on his name do call.

Don't let the world make you rush
And cause you to forget
That I alone have ransomed you;
I paid your sinner's debt.

I did not count the cost that day
I walked Golgotha's path.
I sacrificed my life for you
So that your soul will last.

So, Child of Mine, remember this
Each day, on earth, you trod:
Just calm your heart and remain still
And know that I am God.

BLESSINGS

Father, let me be a blessing;
May all that I meet each day
See in me your Son's true image
As I walk His narrow way.

Father, fill my life with blessings;
May your faithfulness be shown.
May I ever praise you, Father,
For your gifts from heaven's throne.

Father, may I use the blessings
That you've freely given to me
So that those in need will prosper
And your great love for them see.

COME, LIKE LITTLE CHILDREN

*Jesus said, "Let the little children come to
me, and do not hinder them, for the kingdom
of heaven belongs to such as these."*

Come, like little children, who know how big God is.
Come, like little children, and know that you are His.
No thing's too small to ask of God; their faith puts us to shame.
They know the power and might of God and know to call His name.

Come, like little children, and walk up to the throne
Come, like little children, and his great love will be shown.
Just ask of God, expect results, and He will do the rest.
His answer, though it not be ours, will always be for best.

Come, like little children, and sit within his arms.
Come, like little children, and hide away from harm.
His arm of justice will prevail and sinners run and hide.
There is no earthly power that thrives when God is by our side.

Come, like little children, with faith as mustard seed
Come, like little children, in times of fear and need.
And God will listen to our prayers and give divine reply
If we, like little children, on His holy name will cry.

COMFORT THE COMFORTLESS

*Praise be to the God and Father of our Lord Jesus
Christ, the Father of compassion and the God of
all comfort, who comforts us in all our troubles, so
that we can comfort those in any trouble with the
comfort we ourselves have received from God."*

2 Corinthians 1:3-4 NIV

The God who is Father to my Lord, Jesus Christ,
Has shown great compassion to me.
In times of great turmoil, I can call on His name
And His mercy and power I see.
His comfort restores me; I can stand straight and tall
Unbowed by the trials I'd known.
His comfort renews me; all sorrow is gone
By the holy compassion I'm shown.

I, too, must give comfort to those that I meet
Whose troubles and sorrows assail.
To tell them that, with the love of the Father,
Their troubles will never prevail.
To tell them what my God has done in my life
In times of great trials and strife,
How His comfort sustains me throughout all my days
And will continue to the end of my life.

DO UNTO OTHERS

"So in everything, do to others what you would have them do to you, for this sums up the Law and the Prophets."

The Law and the Prophets can be summed up
In a statement that is ever true:
In everything do unto others
As you would have them do unto you.
And even in harsh persecution,
Do not yield yourself up into sin.
Just yield yourself up to the Spirit,
The helper that will help you within.
Don't speak evil words even though they are tossed
At you as you walk every day
Just remember the words that Christ Jesus said
And you'll remain on the narrow way.
And if your enemy's harmed you
And you find that his life has gone wrong,
Do not repay evil for evil
Though the temptation may be very strong.
Instead go ahead and supply him
With all that he needs in his trial.
Your obedience will get you a blessing
And to God's face you'll bring a smile.

FEAR THE LORD

*Charm is deceptive, and beauty is fleeting; but a
woman who fears the LORD is to be praised.*

Proverbs 31:30 NIV

A person with charm is seen by the world
As a person that one needs to know.
But God, in his word, has made it quite clear
The reality is not quite so.
For charm is deceptive and can hide many flaws
Such as guile, betrayal and lust.
You must look ever deeper until you can see
A quality that you can trust.

Beauty is fleeting and only skin deep
And time will just take it away.
True beauty will lie in the heart and the soul
That are living in God's holy way.
A person who fears God should be honored and praised
For the wisdom they show in their life.
With the Lord as their Savior, Redeemer and King
They'll be touched, but unscathed, by their strife.

For the fear of the Lord is knowledge attained,
A goal we must all strive to reach.
This knowledge is found in God's holy word
That will instruct, convict and teach.
So live with the beauty within your heart,
And charm that will help mankind's ills.
Fear the Lord and gain knowledge
As you walk in the Father's pure will.

FOR THE GOOD OF THOSE WHO LOVE HIM

*And we know that in all things God works
for the good of those who love him, who have
been called according to his purpose.*

Romans 8:28 NIV

For the good of those who love him,
Our God works in everything.
This fact we can know for certain
For he is our Lord and King.
All those called out for his purpose
Can avail of his great power
As our God works out his promise
To walk with us through each hour.
His answers will not match up
With what the world decrees,
But we know that it will end well
When his blessed face we see.
So our praises rise to heaven
As his faithfulness is known,
As his grace and love and mercy
To his chosen ones are shown.
And we know that God will work out,
For our good, all of his plans,
And the elected, with their Savior,
Can rise up and heal our land.

GLORIOUS DAY

*For the Lord himself will come down from heaven, with a
loud command, with the voice of the archangel and with
the trumpet call of God, and the dead in Christ will rise
first. After that, we who are still alive and are left will be
caught up together with them in the clouds to meet the
Lord in the air. And so we will be with the Lord forever.*

1 Thessalonians 4:16-17 NIV

The Lord himself will come from heaven,
And with a loud command,
Will usher in a time of peace,
So glorious and grand.

With the voice of the archangel,
And God's holy trumpet call,
The fulfillment of the ages
Will be shown to one and all.

The trumpet of the Lord will sound,
And the dead in Christ shall rise.
Then those believers still on earth
Will join Him in the skies.

We'll join Him in the clouds that day,
No more to leave His side.
The hope we had for many years
Will be completely satisfied.

So, Lord, help me to look ahead
To that great, glorious day,
To share the hope that rules my life
To those on my life's way.

GLORY'S AHEAD

"However, as it is written: 'What no eye has seen, what no ear has heard, and what no human mind has conceived... the things God has prepared for those who love him??

1 Corinthians 2:9 NIV

No eye has seen, no ear has heard,
No mind can e'er conceive
Of all the riches laid in store
For those who will believe.
The jasper walls will shine so bright.
The streets are paved with gold.
The world wars to own such wealth
But it's lifeless, dead and cold.
In heaven, under God's own Son,
The darkness won't attend
For Christ's own righteousness will shine
And will never have an end.
No matter what we have on earth
Of value we hold dear,
In heaven, there will be much more.
The Bible's true and clear.
The life we live on earth today
Is but a second's time,
But there we'll know, in full delight,
God's great love, so sublime.
I walk this earth, and each new day,
I know God's grace and love.
But I will know the full extent
When my soul soars up above.
In sweet communion, I will walk
With God and Christ, my King.
And hear the praise words all around
As with the saints I sing.
And with the time I have left here
I will live but have an eye,
To the time when I can see my Lord
In the sweet, sweet by-and-by.

GOD OF THE IMPOSSIBLE

You are the God of the impossible
The Lord of what cannot possibly be.
When we, as humans, pray in faith to you
Your great miracles we will always see.

No prayer is too little to be answered.
No request too big for you to perform.
Earthly resources you hold in your hand
And the power's in your mighty right arm.

In our way of thinking, the problem's too big
When we do not acknowledge your power.
If we read God's word and know who you are
The victory is ours in that prayerful hour.

For we must not limit you in our time of need
We must offer prayer believing this truth,
That in Christ, believers can do all things.
And in gratitude, lift our praises to you!

GOD'S QUESTIONS

When we stand before God's holy throne,
When our race on earth is run,
God will ask these questions, I am sure,
"Do you know and love my Son?
Do you know He died on Calvary's cross
To rescue your soul from hell?
Do you know His mercy, love and grace?
Did you the Good News tell?
Do you know the peace that fills the soul
When the world tries to win?
Do you remember the feeling you knew
When He cleansed your soul from sin?
Did you read the Word, my blessed Word?
Did you walk His narrow way?
Did you share the love that my Son showed you
To others throughout each day?

I know that if our answer is yes,
His arms will be opened wide,
He'll say, "Welcome home, Child. Enter in
And in my presence, you'll abide."
I know that there will never be tears,
And death no more have reign.
For all time, we'll praise God and his Son
And in their love we'll remain.
I also know if we cannot say yes,
If Christ's not our Savior and King,
Then we'll be cast into hell's roaring fire
And our life of damnation begins.
All hope will be futile; we cannot escape
The fire that never consumes.
We gave up the chance to accept Christ;
That choice sealed our eternal doom.

HOLY AND HUMAN

*Your attitude should be the same as that of Christ
Jesus: Who, being in very nature God, did not consider
equality with God something to be grasped, but made
himself nothing, taking the very nature of a servant,
being made in human likeness. And being found
in appearance as a man, he humbled himself and
became obedient to death— even death on a cross!*

Philippians 2:5-8 NIV

Christ is one with God the Father
And equality is his.
It is not something to be grasped,
But the wondrous part is this –
He took the form of a human man
And came as a helpless babe,
To sin-filled world down here on earth;
All mankind he came to save.

He knew the Father's plan before
He ever came to earth,
That those who would repent and yield
To Christ would gain new birth.
He knew what had to happen here
But Christ counted not the cost,
And became obedient to death –
A death on Calvary's cross.

His death alone does not provide
A way through heaven's door.
For if He'd stayed within the tomb,
We'd be lost forevermore.
But Christ arose on the third day
In glory and in power,
And gives us hope we too will live
Due to that resurrection hour.

We'll live on earth in His great love,
His mercy and His grace
And when we die, we'll slip this earth
And reside in heaven's place.
We'll live in mansions, walk on gold –
I scarcely can comprehend
That daily I will see God's face
And talk as friend-to-friend.

I HEARD YOU CALL FROM CALVARY'S TREE

I heard you call from Calvary's tree,
"Repentant heart, come unto me.
Leave all your sin and shame behind
For all you'll need, in me you'll find.
It matters not how dark the stain;
My blood will cleanse your heart again
And it will be as white as snow.
My grace and peace is all you'll know."

And then I said, "Dear Lord, I fear
That my sin state's not been made clear.
I lived a life of selfish pride
When thoughts of you were pushed aside.
I was the one who held control
Without a thought of my own soul.
Eternal hell held not a part
In my own thinking in my heart."

You said, "I've loved you for so long.
Your way of thinking is all wrong.
The vilest soul that yields his heart
To me will gain a brand new start.
That soul will know my love and grace
And peace will usurp worry's place.
If you alone lived on this earth,
I'd still have died to give you worth."

And then I said, "O Lord above,
I thank you for your gracious love
That lifted me from miry clay
And set me on your narrow way.
You washed me in your precious blood
And I rose cleansed from out that flood.
My soul soars now, alive and free
For I heard you call from Calvary's tree."

I KNOW GOD'S HERE ON EARTH TODAY

I know God's here on earth today,
Not in an earthly form,
But I felt His loving kiss on my cheek
As the wind blew soft and warm.

I know God's here on earth today,
For I've seen his power and might.
The thunder rolled and lightning streaked
Across the sky last night.

I know God's here on earth today,
For I heard the kids at play.
I'm sure it brought a smile to His face
As He passed along the way.

I know God's here on earth today,
The proof's in a newborn's cry -
A gift from God, and tomorrow's hope,
That money cannot buy.

I know God's here on earth today,
For I've seen the mountains grand,
And I know that every inch of them
Was fashioned by His hand.

I know God's here on earth today,
For my soul knows joy and peace.
Each new day brings His blessings
And a love that will not cease.

So, look today around each place
That you find yourself to be,
And I know, without a doubt I know,
That God's presence you will see.

I PRAYED FOR YOU TODAY

I mentioned you in my prayer time.
The Lord remembered your name.
He told of the love that He gifted to you
And that your life was never the same.

I prayed that you hear His soft whispers
In your moments of quiet despair,
That your knowledge of Him will daily increase
As you abide in the Savior's care.

That He'll rejoice with you in your victories,
That on His truth each day you'll stand,
That you'll know in the times of fear and distress
That you're held in the Savior's hand.

I WILL ALWAYS BE WITH YOU

My body feels the pain no more.
I float above the stars.
Although unseen, please always know
I'll be right where you are.

I'll watch the steps you take each day,
And when you think of me,
Just rest assured that I'll be there
Though my body you can't see.

And when the wind blows on your face
So softly, then you'll know
That it is me that's kissing you
My eternal love to show.

And when you feel the sunshine's warmth,
Remember what I've said,
That love still lasts through death's dark door
Though the body may be dead.

And know that I will miss you all:
I know you'll miss me too.
I will live on in memories
That I experienced with you.

So mourn a little, everyone,
But know my spirit's free
And I will always be with you
Though my body you can't see.

IF WE CONFESS OUR SINS

*If we confess our sins, he is faithful and just and will
forgive us our sins and purify us from all unrighteousness.*

1 John 1:9 NIV

If we confess our sins, God is faithful.
If we confess what we've done, he is just.
He has said we will be forgiven.
In God's holy word, we can trust.

If we confess our sins, he will cleanse us
From all unrighteousness and sin.
Our lives will be clean from the inside;
His Spirit will reside within.

If we confess our sins, he will listen
And our sins will be cast in the depths.
Never to be seen and as far apart
As the east is from the west.

So, this really is quite simple.
Just confess your sins to God.
Your life will be cleansed for all the time
That on this earth you trod.

And you'll know the reward for your actions
That just by confessing your sin,
You gained the abundant life promised
And in God's heaven, you'll enter in.

IF WE DON'T LEARN TO LISTEN

If we don't learn to listen
To God's quiet little voice,
And drown out what he's saying
When it's against our choice,
Then our heart will become hardened
And our hearing become weak.
We'll go through life advising
That God doesn't really speak.

If we don't do his bidding
And choose to go our way,
We'll lose this close communion
And not hear what he's got to say.
We'll lose his holy guidance
As he fulfills his divine plan.
Without his daily leading
We'll stumble and won't stand.

But if we choose to listen
As he whispers in our life,
We'll gain the power to conquer
All circumstance and strife.
We'll win the battle daily
With God's words in our ear,
And know that he won't leave us
For he'll be ever near.

And if we choose to listen
To all his loving words,
His guidance and his mercy
Will be our just rewards.
And if we heed his leading
We'll be complete and whole.
We'll always hear the quiet words
He whispers in our soul.

I'M SORRY FOR COMPLAINING, LORD

I'm sorry, Lord, for lack of trust
That caused me to complain.
Help me recall you're in control
And will my life sustain.

I should not question what you do
Or try to second-guess.
When I recall your faithfulness,
You've always done what's best.

I know that grumbling makes you sad,
When I do not let you reign
Within my life I've yielded up,
And I take control again.

I know complaining is a sin
For it means I do not trust
The plan that you've made for my life,
From birth 'til turned to dust.

Please help me be content in all
You've done for me to date.
Help me stay still, with peaceful heart,
As, in your will, I wait.

IT DOES NOT MATTER

No matter how dark your existence was once,
No matter what sin or what shame,
The Lord can forgive and grant new life to you,
If you will but call on His name.

The vilest offender, with repentant heart,
Receives grace and mercy and peace,
A soul that's been washed in the blood of the Lamb
And God's love that will never cease.

The thief on the cross, when he saw Christ as Lord,
Was told, by Christ, he would be
In paradise with that same Jesus Christ
For all of eternity.

So, Friend, if you think that Christ's blood can't atone
For the sins and misdeeds of your past,
Just remember these words, and call out in Christ's name
For the joy and the peace that will last.

IT WAS NOT FAIR

It was not fair you wore the crown
Of cruel thorns upon your brow.
It should be mine, except for grace,
When you stepped in and took my place.

It was not fair that on your back
You wore the scourger's cruel tracks.
Those were the stripes that were my due
But grace and love were shown by you.

It was not fair; you bore the cross
Up Calv'ry's hill to save the lost.
And yet all those you came to save
Yelled "Crucify!"; your blood they craved.

It was not fair you hung and bled
And took my sin upon your head.
You never counted up the cost
To save my soul from heaven's loss.

It was not fair; on the cross you hung
But then you whispered, "It is done".
They laid you in a tomb and then
After three days, you rose again.

Dear Lord, I know it was not fair
That you died for me. I'll e'er declare
The truth of what you did for me
When you hung and bled on Calvary's tree.

LEST WE FORGET

We wear the poppy on our breasts
To recall sacrifice
Of men and women, in the war,
Who paid a grievous price.

They may have died in foreign lands
Or right here on our shore.
They may have come back home again
But were changed forevermore.

The poppy, with its crimson hue,
Recalls the blood that flowed.
It flowers near the graves of those
Whose love for man was shown.

The blackness at the poppy's heart
Recalls the dark and strife
Of all who fight for liberty
And offer up their life.

The poppy with its blackened heart
Helps me recall a man
Who shed his life for man's sin state
According to God's plan.

His blood ran red from grievous wounds
As he hung upon that tree.
He also yielded up his life
For my soul's liberty.

I do not wear an outward sign,
Like poppies on my chest.
I do, however, wear with pride
His name, for He's the best.

His name was Jesus Christ, you see,
He is my Lord and King.
I know, without Him in my life,
I can't do anything.

So when you see a poppy red,
Recall the sacrifice
Of those who loved their brothers true
And paid a grievous price.

But also think of Jesus Christ
Who loved mankind to death-
His death upon Golgotha's hill.
May we daily not forget!

LET THE WORD OF CHRIST DWELL RICHLY

*Let the word of Christ dwell in you richly as you
teach and admonish one another with all wisdom,
and as you sing psalms, hymns and spiritual
songs with gratitude in your hearts to God.*

Colossians 3:16 NIV

Let the word of Christ dwell richly
Within your ransomed heart.
As you admonish each other,
May God's wisdom He impart.
As you teach each other in wisdom,
May you ever do it in praise
In singing psalms and spiritual songs;
To our Father, hymns you'll raise.
For gratitude should swell your heart
For all the Father's done.
He gave for sin-stained man on earth
His holy, precious Son.
Christ knew that Calvary was his fate –
A death so harsh and cruel.
And yet, he yielded up His life
So we, with Him, would rule.
So, daily, raise your hands in praise
And words of thanks give forth,
For God the Father and the Son
Have given your cleansed soul worth.

LITTLE GIRL LOST

I watched the little girl there
As she stood so all alone.
No people walked the darkening street.
She should have been at home.
The tears began to fill her eyes,
And then began to fall.
My heart was gripped by her mischance,
And just when I would call
A man came around the corner,
And saw the child there.
She looked at him with tear-filled eyes
And said, "Daddy, I'm so scared.
I looked around and you were gone.
I looked and looked for you."
"My darling daughter, now you're safe.
I was looking for you, too."
He held his arms wide open
And she ran to be embraced.
What joy they both knew in that time
As he bent and kissed her face.

I was a little girl once
Who was lost and all alone.
I'd lost my way and, by myself,
Could not find my way home.
I felt the terror fill my heart,
For I knew that I was lost.
Where was my help to come from,
And what would be the cost?
And just when I believed that I
Would surely meet my end,
My father came to search for me,
And I saw him round the bend.

He said that he'd been looking for me
Throughout all that time.
What comfort his words gave me
In that fear-filled heart of mine.
He held his arms wide open
And I ran to be embraced.
What joy we both knew in that time
As he bent and kissed my face.

My heavenly father searched for me;
He knew that I was lost.
He sent His own son, Jesus Christ,
To die and pay my cost.
He knew, without that sacrifice
Of blood and shame and pain,
I could never enter heaven
Due to my heart's dark stain.
And when my contrite heart called out,
"O Father, save me now",
My Father heard and came to me
And at His feet I bowed.
I'm now a daughter of the King,
An heir with Jesus Christ
Of God's immense resources.
My praises daily rise
For Christ held His arms open wide,
And I'm held in His embrace.
What joy I will know some day when
I see Him face-to-face.

LORD, HELP ME

Jesus, stop me from becoming attached
To the golden things here on earth.
All of earth's treasures will tarnish and rust
And in eternity won't have worth.

I don't need the gold, the silver or gems;
Their luster holds no great appeal.
Help me discern, with your wisdom, Lord,
What is false and what things are real.

Don't let me focus on what will not last,
All temporal things that will rust.
Instead, help me put my focus on you
And yield my life to you, in trust.

I don't know the future, but this thing I know
You know it all, Lord, start to end.
Help me to remember past days in my life
When you stood by my side as my friend.

So, Lord, as I walk here on earth, day by day,
I know that you will walk beside,
And I'll not be attracted to earth's golden charms
As I daily, in your will, abide.

LORD, YOU ARE

Psalm 145: 8-21

Gracious and compassionate,
Slow to anger, rich in love.
All characteristics of you, Lord,
Who reigns in might above.
The Lord has compassion for all he made,
And we should praise you too
And tell of your kingdom's glory
And the might we find in you.
That all men may know the splendor
Of your everlasting reign,
And throughout all generations,
Our praise will be the same.
The Lord is faithful through all time;
His love to us is shown.
The Lord upholds all those who fall
And all who are bowed down.
The eyes of all look to you, Lord,
And you give us our food
At the proper time, you give it, Lord,
And we know that it is good.
You open wide your hand, Lord,
And the desires of each living thing
Is satisfied with what you give.
Our praises now we sing!
You're righteous, Lord, in all your ways,
And love what you create,
And when we call on your name in truth,
You draw near to us and wait
To hear just what we're asking,
To save us from a fall.
The desires of those who fear you, Lord,
Are fulfilled in you, in all.
I know you watch over those who love you,
But the wicked you destroy.

My mouth will speak in praise of the Lord.
It's my passion and my joy.
And let every creature praise you, Lord,
Always and ceasing never
And may this praise go on throughout the years,
Forever and forever.

LOVE DROPS

And being in anguish, he prayed more earnestly, and his sweat was like drops of blood falling to the ground.

Luke 22: 43-45 NIV

You prayed in Gethsemane's garden,
"Not my will, Father, but thine be done."
By your willing acceptance of God's will
My salvation was already won.
You prayed in that garden in anguish.
So earnest, dear Lord, were your prayers
That your sweat was like drops of blood, Lord.
No thought of yourself did you spare.
And the day that you hung on dark Calvary,
With the crown, made of thorns, on your brow,
From your hands and your feet and side, Lord,
Your precious blood, just for me, flowed down.
You were beaten and scourged and your body
Was abused as you hung on that cross,
But you never once thought to call angels
For you knew then that my soul would be lost.
So, Lord, I would just like to thank you
For the love drops that you've shed for me.
Your death and great resurrection
Cleansed my soul and gave me liberty.
And the blood that you shed there on Calvary,
In a flood of compassion and grace,
Was the price that you paid for my sin, Lord.
In great love, you hung in my place.

LOVE YOUR BROTHER

If anyone says, "I love God," yet hates his brother, he is a liar. For anyone who does not love his brother, whom he has seen, cannot love God, whom he has not seen. And he has given us this command: Whoever loves God must also love his brother."

1 John 4:20-21 NIV

If any man can utter the words
"I truly love you, God",
And yet can hate his brother,
On lieing ground he trods.
If he can hate his brother,
Who's within his very sight,
Then he can't declare his love for God,
Who is unseen on high.
And God has given this command,
An order like no other,
That loving God, we must obey
And always love our brother.
No time, no miles or circumstance
Will cause us to betray
The Father's great command, and so,
We'll walk His narrow way.
We'll look with eyes of God and see
The hurting and the lost
And help them all in time of need,
And tally not the cost.
We'll hear them with the ears of God,
Each cry and tear that's shed,
And tote their burdens, big and small,
As God the Father said.
For we can't do less than our God did,
When He sacrificed His Son
Who went to Calvary for our sin,
And whispered "It is done!"

Who yielded up his life on earth
So glory'd be our gain
Who with His precious blood that flowed
Cleansed every sin-caused stain.
So daily let us love all those
That God brings to our lives
And humbly take the blessing that
Our gracious Father gives.

LOVE YOUR GOD

"Hear, O Israel: The LORD our God, the LORD is one. Love the LORD your God with all your heart and with all your soul and with all your strength."

Deuteronomy 6:4-5 NIV

Hear, O ye people,
Your God's holy words.
And believe in your hearts
That there's only one LORD.
You must love Him and yield up
To Him your whole heart.
And never from His
Holy way ever part.
With all of your soul,
Show Him how much you love
And blessing will flow
From your Father above.
With all of your strength
That to you was a gift
To God, Son and Spirit
Your loud praises lift.
Use the gifts you've been given
When on Him you called
And yielded a heart
That repented of all
The sins that you'd carried
In guilt and in shame.
What a true transformation
When you called on His name!
With the heart that you gave,
Not in part but in whole,
And the strength in your body
And your newly-cleansed soul,
Give to God all the glory
And honour and praise
As you love Him throughout
All your God-ordained days.

MY CHAINS ARE GONE!

My chains are gone! My soul's set free
Because Christ died on Calvary.
His death alone was not what saved;
He wrested victory from the grave.
For when He showed God's awesome power
And rose that resurrection hour,
That's when my soul was saved from hell.
And for eternity, I'll tell
Of Love that hung upon that tree,
And shed His blood for you and me.

My chains are gone! My soul unbound
For life in Jesus Christ I've found.
No more does Satan's deceit bind
And rend me, to Christ Jesus, blind.
No more do doubt and fear assail
For now I know that Christ prevails.
I know that when my Savior's near
Of anything, I need not fear.
For now I know and understand
I'm held within His mighty hand.

My chains are gone! My future's bright
For now I rest within His sight.
I know that He has worked a plan;
It's for my best, I understand.
No matter what the world may say,
I walk with Christ throughout each day.
I'll use what God has given me
To spread Good News to all I see.
And when my work on earth is done,
Eternity's mine with the Father and Son.

MY FATHERS

When I was just a little girl
My father was my rock.
Each day, he'd take me by the hand
And say, "Come, child, let's walk."
We'd walk for miles, my dad and I,
I'd tell him of my world.
He'd listen with a loving ear
Because I was his girl.
I knew when I was with him
That nothing could go wrong,
For when I looked upon my dad
I saw a loving man, so strong.
He said he'd always be right there,
And we would never part.
Though death made light of such a vow,
He still lives within my heart.

My heavenly father's just the same,
We walk and talk for hours.
He is my Rock on which I stand
For I know his mighty power.
I tell him of my life and such
He listens to my prayers.
I know I'm never left alone
For I'm resting in His care.
One father gave me earthly life,
The other second birth,
One father left me, not by choice,
And slipped this poor flawed earth.
My heavenly father will never leave
And this thought makes me glad
That when my soul wings heavenward
I'll be home with my two Dads.

MY PORTION AND MY CUP

LORD, you have assigned me my portion and my cup; you have made my lot secure. You have made known to me the path of life; you will fill me with joy in your presence, with eternal pleasures at your right hand."

Psalm 16: 5, 11 NIV

You have assigned me my portion.
My cup you have also assigned.
My lot is secure; this I know, Lord,
For I am always on your mind.
The life path you have made known, Lord,
Each step by your hand I am led.
When I'm thirsty, you give me your water
And, when I'm hungry, by you I am fed.
Each moment that I'm in your presence,
And there's never a moment I'm not,
You will fill me with joy and contentment
As I walk in your way, all blood-bought.
And your right hand of bounteous provision
Will provide me with all that I need,
And eternal pleasures you'll give me
If your commands I choose to keep.

MY SIN

My sin yelled "Barabbas"
With the rest of the crowd.
And "Crucify Jesus";
Our voices rose loud.

My sin applied
The thorn crown to your brow.
My sin rejoiced
As the blood drops flowed down.

My sin drove the nails
Through your hands and your feet
My sin laughed and sneered
As you fell in the street.

But your love overrode that
And you reached down from the cross.
I stood in your shadow
A soul no longer lost.

MY TEARS

At the time my soul knew only darkness,
And it felt like no other was near,
It was then, when no words could be uttered,
That Jesus, you read all my tears.

The pain in my soul could not be voiced;
The words in my head all unclear.
But, you loved me and drew close beside me
And you understood all of my tears.

You knew that the pain could not be borne
And in my mind rested trouble and fears,
But you knew what it was I was needing,
And Jesus you dried up my tears.

You said, "Precious child, I so love you.
And I'll be with you throughout your years.
Lean on me for the strength you are needing.
I'll exchange songs of joy for your tears.

NO CONDEMNATION NOW I DREAD

*Therefore, there is now no condemnation for
those who are in Christ Jesus, because through
Christ Jesus the law of the Spirit who gives life has
set you free from the law of sin and death."*

Romans 8:1-2 NIV

No condemnation now I dread
For I am found in Christ.
I will not suffer what I should
For Christ has paid the price.
No fear of death stirs up my soul
For when my life's at end,
I know eternity is mine
With Jesus Christ, my Friend.
The law no longer guides my life
And death no more has power.
For Jesus took back that control
In His resurrection hour.
The Spirit's now my only guide;
His law has set me free
From sin and all its consequence
And granted liberty.
So as I live out each new day
By the Holy Spirit led,
I stand assured salvation's mine;
There's no condemnation's dread.

PARADOX

Because you wore a crown of thorns
A crown of gold I'll see.
Because you died on Calvary
My soul has been set free.
Because you paid the penalty,
My debt is paid and gone.
Salvation's start on Calvary
Began with "It is done".
My soul is now as white as snow
Because your blood ran red.
The words of scorn that I deserved
Fell on your holy head.

These thoughts seem incongruent,
But the truth is very plain.
Because you yielded up your life
I was given birth again.
A birth into abundant life
Replete with joy and peace,
A life where each new day I know
A love that will not cease.
Because, to you, I gave my heart
Quiet assurance fills my soul,
That because you died and rose again
My soul is clean and whole.

REDEEMING CONVERSATION

Jesus said to her, "I am the resurrection and the life.
He who believes in me will live, even though he dies;

John 11:25 NIV

"I am the resurrection and the life",
A preacher said one day.
"All who call upon my name
Will live, though earthly shells decay.
All power in heaven is given to me
By my Father up on high.
And what I say will come to pass.
They'll live though bodies die."

"What mystery is found in you
Where those who pass away
Will live with life eternal
Though their bodies will decay?
I cannot understand it.
It doesn't make much sense.
O, Preacher, please explain it
So that I can comprehend."

"O, Daughter, don't be troubled
For the answer is quite clear.
I love my own creation.
I hold them all quite dear.
I know that man is sinful,
And heaven will be his loss.
Unless a sacrifice is made –
I'll go to Calvary's cross."

Again my thoughts were muddled.
I could not take it in.
I heard this preacher saying
That he would bear man's sin.
And then my heart repented
And I could not help but say,
"O, Preacher, tell me more of this.
Show me the only way."

"O, Daughter, I have heard your heart.
You now belong to me.
Abide in me and love mankind.
Your faith has set you free."
Obey my laws and read my Word,
For it will be your guide.
And I will never leave you.
I'll be right by your side."

My heart was overfilled with joy;
I knew his love and grace.
I saw the love for all mankind
Reflected in His face.
His love and mercy cleared the debt
That I could never pay.
"He is my Christ Redeemer.
The Truth! The Life! The Way!"

SINGING, SHOUTING, PRAISING

*Come, let us sing for joy to the LORD; let us shout aloud
to the Rock of our salvation. Let us come before him
with thanksgiving and extol him with music and song.*

Psalm 95:1-2 NIV

Come, let us sing to the Lord full of joy
And to the Rock let us give a loud shout
He granted salvation to us without charge;
Our lives have been changed, without doubt.
Let's come before him with thanks and with praise.
Let's extol him with music and song.
For the one who created our lives in his plan
Should know that to him we belong.
Let no man have a doubt when our lives he does see
That allegiance is owed to our God.
May our lips always praise him for what he has done
As each day on this earth we do trod.

TEMPTATION

*No temptation has seized you except what is
common to man. And God is faithful; he will not
let you be tempted beyond what you can bear.
But when you are tempted, he will also provide a
way out so that you can stand up under it."*

1 Corinthians 10:13 NIV

No temptation has seized you
Except what is known
To man in his sin state,
But you're not alone.
For our God is faithful
And we rest in His care.
He won't let us be tempted
Beyond what we'll bear.
But Satan won't give up,
And each day he'll try
To tempt us to sin more
By using some lies.
He'll show us the world
Doesn't walk in God's way,
And if we want to do something,
Then it's really okay.
He'll make all of sin
Seem so pleasing and right.
But our weapon is Jesus,
His power and might.
For when we are tempted,
We know we can stand
For the way of escape
Is shown by His hand.
He'll always provide
A way through the trial.
Our daily obedience
Will make Jesus smile.

So, Satan, bring on
All your wiles and your games!
We'll see you defeated
When we call on Christ's name.

THE LIFE LINE

Therefore God exalted him to the highest place and gave him the name that is above every name, that at the name of Jesus every knee should bow, in heaven and on earth and under the earth, and every tongue acknowledge that Jesus Christ is Lord, to the glory of God the Father.

Philippians 2:9-11 NIV

All the nations will be gathered before him, and he will separate the people one from another as a shepherd separates the sheep from the goats. He will put the sheep on his right and the goats on his left. Then the King will say to those on his right, 'Come, you who are blessed by my Father; take your inheritance, the kingdom prepared for you since the creation of the world. … Then he will say to those on his left, 'Depart from me, you who are cursed, into the eternal fire prepared for the devil and his angels.

Matthew 25: 32-34, 41 NIV

I stepped up to a great long line.
I wondered where it led.
I wondered where the line began
For I could not see ahead
Some folks were dressed in filthy rags
And some dressed in finest clothes
While others dressed in common garb
Like you and me, I suppose.
All ages filled the growing line –
Young and old and in between.
There were skins of many colors.
It was quite an amazing scene!
As I approached the long line's start,
I saw pearly gates, so grand.
I saw the King upon His throne
With something in His hand.
I watched as each one neared the throne
And then fell on bended knee,
They proclaimed Christ as Lord of all,
By choice or involuntarily.

He opened up the book He held
And checked for each one's name.
He indicated right or left;
The result was always the same.

If in the Book of Life was found
The name of the bowed soul,
God said, "Go to the right, my child.
Welcome. Now you are at home."
The sheep on the right were given
The kingdom that had been prepared.
Throughout eternity, they'd rest within
The Father's loving care.
But if that person's name was not
Found in the book God held,
Then to the left that person went.
His future would not go well.
"Depart from me, you who are cursed,
Into the eternal flames."
God's words would seal the fate of those
Who, on earth, would not proclaim
That Jesus Christ, God's only son,
Was King and repent of their sins,
Who never knew the peace and joy
Of a soul cleansed from within.
So, decide now which way you'll go
When you near the Judgment seat.
Will you go left with all the goats
Or right with God's own sheep?

THE LORD'S SIGN

Therefore the Lord himself will give you a sign:
The virgin will be with child and will give birth
to a son, and will call him Immanuel.

Isaiah 7:14 NIV

The LORD himself will give a sign –
A virgin will give birth.
The Son of God and Son of Man
Will come to lowly earth.
Within a stable, cold and crude,
His first cries will arise
And heavenly angels overhead
Will fill the midnight skies.
The shepherds who had heard the choir
Will come on bended knee.
And bow, in true humility,
When the Christ Child they first see.
And wise men, coming from the east,
Will come from lands afar
Will bring Him presents, and report
They were led by shining star.
His name would be Immanuel
Which means that God's with us.
And Savior of his people –
His name will be Jesus.
And though it's hard to understand
How a baby, oh so wee,
Could love all people with such love
That He'd die on Calvary.
And never count the cost because
He knew it was God's plan.
He shed His blood on Calvary's cross
To redeem sin-stained man.
And now I know that without Christ,
My life would not have worth.
Forever I will praise the day
When my Savior came to earth.

THE PRAYER OF A RIGHTEOUS MAN

*Therefore confess your sins to each other and pray
for each other so that you may be healed. The prayer
of a righteous man is powerful and effective.*

James 5:16 NIV

The prayer of a righteous man
Is effective and has power,
No matter what the circumstance,
No matter what the hour.
And when that man begins to pray
And all his sins confess,
Then God will know and bless that man
For all his righteousness.
You, too, go out and do the same,
Confess your sins and pray.
And you will see the power of God,
If in His will you stay.
Pray for others and yourself;
Include your enemies too.
They may not change but you will feel
A change inside of you
And rancor will not fill your soul,
And your heart will be at peace.
For when you show the love of God,
Your joy will just increase.

54

THE SHEPHERD BOY AND THE SAVIOR

The little shepherd boy walked up
To the manger where Christ lay.
He'd heard the talk of a Savior
And the part that Christ would play.
He'd heard the angel chorus sing
As they told of the new King's birth,
How this baby came from heaven
To save mankind on earth.
As he peeked over the manger,
And saw the infant small,
He couldn't see how this little babe
Could be a King at all.
No servants waited on his needs;
No royal robes were worn.
No palace here for his royal birth,
Just a stable all forlorn.
How could a baby, new and small,
Be the savior of all men?
How could this child of lowly birth
Be the one that God had sent?
But then the baby looked at him,
And the love shone through His eyes.
He saw just what the angels meant
With their announcement in the skies.
The little shepherd boy then knew
This babe would grow to a man,
He'd die and rise again to fulfill
God's great salvation plan.
What joy then filled the little boy,
For he knew that he had seen
The Savior of all men on earth.
His rejoicing was so keen!
He ran with the other shepherds
Throughout the quiet town,
Proclaiming with all of their hearts
That God's Son from heaven came down.

THE SHEPHERDS' FIRST CHRISTMAS

We rested on the hillside grass
And watched our flocks of sheep.
The night was all around us
And it was dark and deep.

We knew, although they weren't seen,
There were lions, wolves and bears.
We knew they'd snatch a wayward lamb
If we didn't stay aware.

And then we heard an angel choir
Proclaim a royal birth.
They said in little Bethlehem
A king had come to earth.

The light shone bright around us;
We all were much afraid
For we had not seen such a thing
In all our combined days.

The angels told us not to fear
For they had news to tell –
A baby born in Bethlehem
Would save mankind from hell.

They said the baby would be found
In a stable all forlorn,
All wrapped up in some swaddling clothes
To keep him dry and warm.

We had to see this for ourselves,
So the sheep were roused from sleep
And we all went to Bethlehem,
This newborn king to see.

And when we reached the stable,
The bright star stayed overhead.
We saw the royal baby
Upon his straw-filled bed.

We bowed down and adored him;
We could not do much else.
And then we ran to tell the world;
We couldn't keep it to ourselves.

We wondered why we shepherds,
Who were despised and set apart,
Would be the chosen group to hear
The good news from the start.

We were humbled and so grateful
That the angels came to us
And told us of earth's Savior King,
And his birth so glorious.

And all the world would hear the tale
Of shepherds in their fields
Who heard the angels, saw the star,
Throughout the coming years.

THE WEDDING MIRACLE

Nearby stood six stone water jars, the kind used by the Jews for ceremonial washing, each holding from twenty to thirty gallons. Jesus said to the servants, "Fill the jars with water" ; so they filled them to the brim. Then he told them, "Now draw some out and take it to the master of the banquet." They did so, and the master of the banquet tasted the water that had been turned into wine. He did not realize where it had come from, though the servants who had drawn the water knew. Then he called the bridegroom aside and said, "Everyone brings out the choice wine first and then the cheaper wine after the guests have had too much to drink; but you have saved the best till now."

John 2: 6-10 NIV

The wedding feast was half-way through
When we ran out of wine.
My master would be shamed if we
Could not an answer find.
Then Mary and her son came near;
She told us what to do:
"Just listen to my Son, Jesus,
And do all he asks of you."

He pointed to the six stone jars
And said, "Fill them to the brim."
The jars were quickly filled up full,
Just as we were told by him.
He told us draw from out the jars,
And to the banquet master go.
Why would this man send servants
With plain water? Who could know?

And when the banquet master drank,
We scarce believed his words.
He said the water turned to wine;
That thought was so absurd.
How could the water we had poured
In jars be turned to wine?
And then we fully understood
It was a miracle divine.

For Jesus, who'd commanded us,
Had a miracle performed.
When something truly common-place
Had divinely been transformed
Into a thing of value rare.
We'd heard the master's words,
That the wine was of the very best,
As he neared the wedding lord.

"Most folks use up the finest wine
At the start, then use the rest.
But you've done things the other way;
At the end you served the best.
You've saved the best wine for the last,
A practice never known
And now the best wine you bring out
Your hospitality to show.

We spoke of all these things and when
We finished, then we knew
That Jesus was the Son of God
And we knew what we should do.
We yielded up our hearts to Him,
And from that moment there,
Our lives, so common-place 'til then,
Became lives, pure and rare.

For that, we later came to know,
Was what Christ would always do –
A sinner, sin-stained and unclean,
Was given life renewed
When, with repentant heart, one came
To fall at Calvary's cross
Where fear was changed for faithfulness,
And diamonds came from dross.

THE WISE AND THE STRONG

The wise man should not boast of his wisdom.
The strong man should not boast of his might.
A man who will humbly give credit to God,
Is a precious jewel in His sight.

For whatever a person possesses,
And whatever a man calls his own
Is a gift of God, acknowledged or not,
And in it, God's great love's always shown.

Never boast that you're better than others.
Never say that there's none with your might.
As quick as the gift was bestowed upon you,
It can vanish in the blink of an eye.

Those who are not quite as wise as you seem,
And those who don't have the same power
Have need to rely on God's wisdom and strength
Through each day and throughout every hour.

They trust in His love, and His mercy and grace,
For they know they are nothing alone.
It is then in their weakness, God's work can be done
And his faithfulness is always shown.

You men of great wisdom and of great strength,
Just consider the source of your gifts
And acknowledge the Lord as the source of them all.
It's the only right way you can live.

THROUGH HIS BLOOD

I know that I can't understand
What made Christ hang on Calvary's tree.
And yet I know that through His blood,
My soul knows glorious liberty.

Through His blood, I stand redeemed
A sinner with a new heart cleaned.

Through His blood, I know His grace
For Christ was crucified in my place.

Through His blood on Calvary's tree,
I've gained salvation, rich and free.

Through His blood, my chains are gone.
I was freed at resurrection's dawn.

Through His blood, I now can claim
His promises, all on His name.

Through His blood, I've joy and peace
And love I know will never cease.

Through His blood, and by His love
I've gained a home in heaven above.

Through His blood, I know I've found
A robe, a mansion and a crown.

I know that I can't understand
What made Christ hang on Calvary's tree.
And yet I know that through His blood,
I'll praise him for soul's liberty.

TRUE FORGIVENESS

For I will forgive their wickedness and
will remember their sins no more.

Jeremiah 31:34 NIV

I neared your holy throne of grace,
Unsure of what might be.
Would you reject me, turn aside,
So that your face I could not see?
Would you heap scorn upon my head,
For I knew my sin-stained state?
Would I be told there is no hope
For repentance came too late?
Would you, the holy righteous one,
Accept my contrite heart?
Would you apply your healing love
To each tiny sin-filled part?
I waited, Lord, with anxious thoughts,
To see what you would do,
And then you took me in your arms
And gave me life renewed.
You told me that you loved me so;
That you'd died, my soul to save,
And then you said the sins I'd brought
Were cast into the waves.
You said that they'd be seen no more;
Their charge on me was gone.
And then you promised that each day
I'd never walk alone.
So, Lord, help me to remember
That forgiveness is your way.
Then I can forgive others
That I meet throughout each day.

WALK TO REDEMPTION

I walked up to the blood-stained cross
Nothing of worth within my hands;
I only had my sin and shame.
Would Jesus ever understand
How my heart yearned to be set free
From Satan's ever tight'ning snare?
Would he accept my contrite heart
Has longed to rest within his care?
I looked upon his bloodied face,
And saw within his eyes of love,
Compassion for my sin-stained soul
That longed to soar to heights above.
With labored breath, I heard him say,
"Come to the cross and no more sin.
I'll take your dross, turn it to gold,
And cleanse your soul from deep within.
You'll be a child of Christ, the King.
And when you call upon my name,
All things will then to you be given.
Your life will never be the same."
I took my Savior at his word,
And then and there my sin confessed.
His peace and joy o'erflowed my soul,
I'm happy now. My soul's at rest.
And yet, there's something I must do
I have to tell the world's lost
That Christ, in love, gave up his life
And not once did he count the cost.
I have to tell them they can gain
The peace and love that fill my soul.
That sin-dark hearts are made as new,
And desperate lives can be made whole.

WARDROBE CHANGE

As I approached your blood-stained cross,
I feared what you would do,
That my tattered suit of sin and guilt
Would not appeal to you,
That the filthy rags of doubt and fear
That hung upon my frame,
Would bring me condemnation,
Disgrace, rejection, shame.
The hat of sin upon my head
Was dirty and threadbare.
Would you accept me as I was
Or condemn me standing there?
You reached down from the cross that day;
And as I held my breath,
The words you said to me that day
Were words of life, not death.
"Come, Child, I love you and you'll be
Availed of my great power.
You'll never walk alone, my Child,
For I'll walk with you each hour."
You took my tattered rags from me,
And replaced them with a robe,
A robe of your own righteousness
That gave new life and hope.
That hat of sin was soon replaced
With a shining, golden crown.
My heart that had repented there
Was cleansed; I was reborn.
You also gave me peace and joy,
And took the doubt and fear,
For naught on earth can harm me
When I know you're standing near.
I know I cannot thank you well
For the gifts you gave to me,
But I know I'll ever praise you
Now and throughout eternity.

WHAT A FRIEND!

What a friend I have in Jesus!
What a friend I have in you!
Your deep love of my friend, Jesus,
Cannot help but shine right through.

You, my friend, are truly gifted
Recognizing each one's need,
Quick to give a word to build up,
Quick to show God's love in deed.

What a blessing I've been gifted
Just to call you my dear friend!
What a comfort I've in knowing
That on you I can depend.

So, I pray that I'll be able
To be seen in that same light
By the folks I meet around me
Who are precious in God's sight.

Just as time with Christ is precious,
So my time with you I see.
When He gave your friendship to me,
I full know that God loves me.

WHAT LOVE DOES

Love does not delight in evil but rejoices with the truth. It always protects, always trusts, always hopes, always perseveres. Love is patient, love is kind. It does not envy, it does not boast, it is not proud. It is not rude, it is not self-seeking, it is not easily angered, it keeps no record of wrongs.

1 Corinthians 13: 4-7 NIV

Love doesn't delight in evil,
But rejoices with the truth.
For love gives its best to the loved one
As God's word says it should.
Love always protects and ever trusts.
It hopes and perseveres.
It does not boast and is not proud
And love drives out all fears.
Love does not envy or cause great harm
And love is never rude.
Love seeks to strive to give its best
For its own beloved's good.
Love is not easily angered;
No record of wrongs are kept.
Love does not seek its own rewards
And rebuke it will accept.
And Christ is our example
Of what true love's about.
He loved us so he died a death-
A cruel death, no doubt.
He selflessly gave his life up
To die on Calvary's tree,
To ensure eternal salvation.
He did this for you and me.
So, let's not forget his anguish
And let's not forget his pain,
Because of what he did for us
Eternity is our gain.

And let us ever follow
The way Christ said we should
And love our God and neighbour too
And only bring them good.

WHOM DO I HAVE IN HEAVEN?

*Whom have I in heaven but you? And earth has nothing
I desire besides you. My flesh and my heart may fail, but
God is the strength of my heart and my portion forever.*

Psalm 73:25-26 NIV

Whom do I have up in heaven
But you, my Lord and my King?
All my desire is for you
And this earth does not offer a thing.

For what could this earth choose to offer
But silver, and diamonds and gold?
The silver and gold will just tarnish
And diamonds are lifeless and cold.

The greater reward would be living
In the presence of Jesus, my Lord
As we share in that quiet communion
That I know as I study His word.

Though my flesh and my heart may falter,
Yet God is the strength of my heart.
He is my portion forever
And from His love, I'll never depart.

WORDS OF LOVE FROM A KING

What do I do with the words of love
That the King of Kings professes?
Do I say, "Lord, you've made a mistake.
Don't you know about all of my messes?"

When I read the Bible, each chapter and verse,
And read all He said about love,
Do I say, "I'm just a woman of earth,
And you are a King from above?"

Or does my heart take flight at the sound of His voice,
As He whispers love words in my ear?
Does the sound of his voice, and profound words of love,
Cast away any remnant of fear?

Do I run to my Lord with my arms open wide,
As His arms are held out to me?
Do I wait for the time in each twenty-four hours
When together with my Loved One I'll be?

Do I shout to the world that I'm loved by the Lord?
Do I tell that He'll never forsake?
Do I do all the things so the lost souls will know
That He died on the cross for their sake?

For I know without doubt that the words that He speaks
Are true, and are meant just for me,
And I'll stay in His arms, in His loving embrace,
Here on earth and for eternity.

WRAPPED IN MYSTERY

The secret of the Lord is with them that fear him.

Psalm 25:14

There are secrets of Providence
That God's children learn
That those who don't know God
Can never discern.
What seems like a hardship
Shines brightly with hope.
With God right beside them,
Believers can cope.
For faith looks much deeper
And is able to see
The gold that is wrapped up
In God's mystery.
With faith, we can hang in
And come out the end
Of each trial and trouble;
Our faith will not bend.
Our steps will not falter;
We'll finish the race
Sustained by our God's love,
His mercy and grace.
And in each time of trouble,
We'll find something new
To remind in the future
Of His faithfulness, true.
Great treasure awaits us;
In wisdom we rise
And claim victory in Jesus
And the gold is our prize.
The bright gold of wisdom
And knowledge we'll gain,
For no value is put on
A prize without pain.

YOU ARE MY ONLY CONSTANT

God, you are the only constant
That I have in my life,
For man may leave and me forsake
In times of fear or strife.
I know that you'll walk with me
And never leave my side
If I but walk your narrow way
And in your love abide.

Your promises don't change, Lord,
For they are ever true.
No matter what the circumstance,
I know that you are you –
A god of mighty power and love,
Of mercy and of grace.
A god whose spoken word commanded
Earth to form in space.

Your love is never ending,
No conditions do you voice
That need be met before a sinner
Can repent and then rejoice
For the new life that you give, LORD,
And dark sins all atoned.
No other god could do this, LORD.
No, only God alone.

Your word will be my guidepost,
As daily I remain
In all your love and mercy,
Wthout sin's dark, dark stain.
My praises will soar upward
Onto heaven's holy throne.
You are my only constant.
I belong to you alone.

YOU CALLED ME

Lord, you called me to Calvary
In a voice meek and mild
And said, "My arms are wide open.
Come to Calvary, my child"
And bring me all of your troubles
Your guilt and all your shame
And I will cleanse and renew you
In my Father's holy name.
Drag your doubts and fears behind you
And leave them at the cross.
For I'll give you life abundant
To replace all of the dross.
Please know your past does not matter;
Your new life can now start
When you near the cross of Calvary
With a true repentant heart.
My blood that dropped on Calvary
Will cleanse your soul within
And you will be a child of God
When I forgive your sins."
I listened with great amazement
My soul filled with delight.
I gave you all my heart and soul
And experienced your might.
I see the world in a different light.
Now that I am set free.
No longer Satan's sin-bound slave,
Your Spirit lives in me.
I never can repay you, dear Lord,
For what you've done for me.
I am glad I listened to your voice
When you called from Calvary.

YOU COULD HAVE

You could have said you knew my worth
Was much less than the cost,
But you hung and bled on Calvary's cross
For without that, I was lost.

You could have said I'd made my choice
And deserved all that I got,
But you never said a word of blame
As you, my redemption bought.

You could have called angelic hordes
To take you from that tree.
But you kept in mind the Father's will
And took my place, for love of me.

You could have said the pain's too great
In that dark forsaken hour,
But you looked ahead, with thoughts of me,
To your resurrection power.

And there's nothing I can do or give
That is ample recompense
Except to yield my heart and soul.
It all makes perfect sense.

For all you suffered on Calv'ry's tree,
For all that you've done and will do,
My heart and soul can't really compare
But they both belong to you.

YOU COULD HAVE, AND YET

You could have left me in my sin,
Without eternity to win.
You could have said I had no worth
And stayed in heav'n; not come to earth.
You could have said, "I cannot bear
The burden of the crown I'll wear."
You could have said, "The cross is tough;
Of salvation's plan, I've had enough."
You could have said "I'll not be born
In a manger stall on Christmas morn."
You could have said "A palace grand
Should be my place in my Father's plan".
And yet, you stayed in God's own will
And came to Bethlehem, so still.
That Christmas morning, you were born
In a lowly stable, so forlorn.
No servants bowed, no palace grand.
Just shepherds who knew angels sang.
No bed piled high to lay your head
For a manger was your holy bed.
That Christmas morning long ago
Began the saving of my soul.
Your death on Calvary's cruel cross
Ensured my soul would not be lost.
I know I'll never understand
Why you agreed to God's own plan,
And in submission, died a death
On Calvary's tree - you hung and bled.
You died, were buried, Lord, and then
In power and might, you rose again.
And sealed the fate of death and grave,
As mankind's sinful soul you saved.
All those whose true repentant hearts
Will call on you, new lives will start.
They'll thank you, Lord, as well they should
That you did not do all you could.

YOU DID IT ALL FOR ME

You hung there bleeding in my place
And thus bestowed on me your grace.
You hung there on that wooden cross
So that my soul would not be lost.
You wore a crown of painful thorns
So that my soul could be reborn.
They pierced your hands, your side, your feet
So that my soul would be made clean.
They mocked you, Lord, and scorned your name
But now I can your promise claim.
They used the scourge to stripe your back;
My soul turned white from sin-stained black.
They beat you 'til you could not see
And yet you hung and bled for me.

They tried to kill you; this I know
And yet your power would not be shown
Until that resurrection hour
When you displayed your divine power.
The stone was rolled away and then
You rose in power to live again
So those who call on your dear name
Will never, ever be the same.
A heart, repentant of its sin
Will bow and ask its Savior in
To cleanse and to restore as new
The soul that's yielded up to you.
And then your grace and love they'll see
As they live lives of liberty.

YOU KNEW

You knew that when you came to earth,
A manger'd be your bed.
You knew a stable so forlorm
Was where you'd lay your head.
No kingly garments would you wear;
No gold would you possess.
And yet you chose to come to earth
To be man's righteousness.

You knew that to a man you'd grow.
And when all was said and done,
You knew those Nazarenes would not
Regard you as God's Son.
"Is this not Joseph's son?", they'd ask.
With sneering voice and tone.
And yet you chose to come to earth
So man's sins could be atoned.

You knew that on Golgotha's cross
You'd hang in scorn and shame.
You knew the people would deride.
Your holy precious name.
You'd know your Father'd turn away
From all the sins you bore.
And yet you chose to come to earth
To open heaven's door.

You knew that you'd be buried then
And lay in death's dark hands
For three days, then you'd rise again
To fulfill salvation's plan.
You knew your resurrection hour
Would save sinners, just like me.
That's why you chose to come to earth
And fulfilled all prophecy.

I'm humbled by the knowledge that
You knew what lay ahead,
And yet, in love, you came to earth
And hung there in my stead.
With humble heart of gratitude,
I thank you, Lord, in praise.
I'll thank you for salvation's gift
Throughout my earthly days.

YOU KNEW IT ALL

You knew the pain of the scourger's strike;
You knew the cross's heavy weight.
You knew the sound of the hammer on nails
On that pain-filled crucifixion date.
You knew the pain of betrayal
When a disciple went astray.
You knew the sense of desolation
When God turned his face away.
You knew your mother's broken heart
As she watched you hanging bruised.
You knew the pain when soldiers
Your *King of the Jews* title abused.
I know that I can't understand –
My mind won't ever comprehend –
Why you would leave your glory throne
And on earth meet such an end.
You knew what you were headed for
When, as a babe, you came to earth.
Your pain-filled sacrifice, for me,
Ensured my eternal worth.
And though you knew the pain you'd feel,
You willingly took my place
As a sin-filled sinner who ought to die.
You showed great mercy and grace.
But you also knew the promise
Of resurrection that Easter morn,
So those that call upon your name
Would have their souls reborn.
Because you knew it all, Lord,
And yet you chose to come,
Help me to let the lost sheep know
And find their right way home
Into the arms of Jesus Christ,
The savior of their souls,
The one, whose blood on Calvary,
Gives life and makes them whole.

And let me always praise you for
My second birth by your grace,
For life renewed and cleansed within
By your taking this sinner's place.
I know that I can never repay
The debt you paid that day
When all the sins of mankind
Were on your shoulders laid.
And the greatest thought that comes to mind
Is that you left your throne above
And even knowing your pain-filled end,
You came to earth in love.

YOUR MAJESTIC NAME

*O Lord, our Lord, how majestic is
your name in all the earth!*

Psalm 8 :1 NIV

O Lord, our Lord! Your majestic name
Is in all the earth, and your people proclaim
That our God's the real God; no other's the same.

You ordained that children and infants give praise
Forever and ever, throughout all the days,
To silence your enemies and their evil ways.

When I look 'round and see what you've done-
The moon and the stars, the bright shining sun-
I lift up my praise for the true Holy One.

What is man that the Lord is so mindful of him,
When his heart is so evil and covered in sin?
Yet, Christ died on the cross his salvation to win!

You made man just lower than the angels on high
And gave him dominion over all things that fly
In your great creation, in the heavenly sky.

Over all of the flocks and the herds, he has reign
Over all of creation that you did ordain.
All praise and glory to your majestic name!

O Lord, our Lord! Your majestic name
Is in all the earth, and your people proclaim
That our God's the real God; no other's the same.

YOUR NAME CAME TO MY MIND TODAY

Your name came to my mind today,
And I mentioned you in prayer.
I asked the Lord to keep you safe
As you rest within His care.
I asked that you would feel His love,
A love that knows no end.
I prayed you'd know, no matter what,
On Him you can depend.
I prayed that you would daily know
His power and His might
That is all times availed to you
To make the wrong things right.
I prayed that you would lean on Him
For all that you would need,
And all His great abundance
From Him you would receive.
I prayed that you'd be thankful
For all that He's bestowed,
And that the love you get from Him
To others will be shown.
I prayed that you'd experience
His mercy, love and grace
Throughout each mountain moment
And when in the valley place.
And then I prayed you'd always know
Though I cannot be right there,
That when your name comes to my mind,
I will mention you in prayer.

YOUR WORD

Your word is true, Lord.
There is nothing that could happen to make it untrue.
There is nothing that could change its meaning.

Your word is clear, Lord.
There is no ambiguity in its meaning.
There is no doubting its authenticity.

Your word is constant, Lord.
There is no situation in present or past history that it did not cover.
There is no future event to which it would not apply.

Your word is life-changing, Lord.
There is no life that cannot be transformed by your word.
There is no keeping this change to oneself when it happens
to a person.

Your word is a lifeline, Lord.
There is no situation I could encounter where it would not
sustain me.
There is no place or time where it is not accessible to me.

Thank you, Lord, for the wondrous gift of your word.